Finding My Voice

By

Benjamin K. M. Kellogg

Finding My Voice

By

Benjamin K. M. Kellogg

© 2020

Published by Ex-L-Ence Publishing a division of Winghigh Limited, England.

The right of Benjamin K. M. Kellogg to be identified as the author of this work has been asserted by him in accordance with the Copyright, Designs and Patents Act 1998.

ISBN: 978-1-9164944-4-2

Contents

Dedication

This book is dedicated to Mrs. Michelle Sanz and Ms. Jacqueline Bates, two of my childhood speech teachers who have become great friends in my adult years. These poems, and many other aspects of my life, would not have been possible without their devotion to me. Thank you for helping me to develop the communication skills needed to speak my mind clearly and confidently, engage with my family, friends, and community, and find my voice.

About the Author

Benjamin K. M. Kellogg, 29, is a freelance writer with autism, currently residing in a small town in Central New York, USA, where he has lived with his parents his entire life.

In his understanding of the autism condition, it means his brain is wired differently, which has carried with it a host of physical, mental, and psychological considerations he must negotiate every day. His every life decision, from daily care and diet, to activity choices, to maintaining social niceties when interacting with people, must be carefully considered, informed by years of experience and a personal drive to do his best. Autism, quite literally, informs every aspect of his existence, and he has become well aware of how acutely it plays a role in his ability to function and make his own decisions.

Benjamin's intention with this collection of poems is to offer readers insight regarding his life with autism. Each poem reflects challenging parts of his average day or significant ones from his past, and his thought process during each. He hopes readers will find insight, inspiration, and entertainment throughout.

Hearing

By now, I have had many opportunities to reflect on how autism affects me.

I was not always as aware.

But I did know, when I was very young, that some things upset me terribly, and they could hurt me, too.

For instance, there were many times when everything seemed perfectly quiet to everyone other than me.

I would suddenly scream and cover my ears. My mom would ask me what was wrong, but I did not have the words to tell her.

Even if I could have found the words, I was not entirely certain what was hurting me.

It took my mom some time to realize I could somehow clearly hear trucks barreling down the highway, engines rumbling, horns blasting, even though we lived a few blocks away from this direct traffic, and where they seldom ever roamed.

Even the tiniest sounds hurt and upset me, like the refrigerator humming, my parents having a conversation in the other room, one of our TVs playing on low volume; really, just about any noise which my ears could detect was virtually impossible for me to ignore.

It turned out, the doctor said, that my auditory functioning was extremely acute and hypersensitive.
I would require special "auditory processing therapy" to help my brain process all that noise.
As time passed, I noticed something wonderful.
I no longer felt nervous or hurt in loud places. I could handle the classroom, the grocery store, the playground, the movie theater; any place where people generated noise.
This therapy vastly improved the quality of my life.

A Day with Autism

I wake up with the sun.
I do get some sleep at night, but it has always taken me some time before I feel even remotely sleepy at night.
From that point on, I like to follow a somewhat orderly schedule.
Of course, I know that's not always possible, but I generally prefer certain things to happen at certain reliable times.
After I get out of bed, making it up ever so carefully so that it looks like I was never there, I shave and shower.
A prime concern is finishing my shower in an appropriately speedy manner to ensure that I do not collapse from the heat.
I like hot showers, but I have fainted a few times, so, I know I need to be careful.
Breakfast is a fantastic balancing act.
Can I make my meal, put it on a tray, and transport it to my preferred dining area without spilling anything?
Lunch and dinner are minor variations of the same, except I do not usually make my own dinner.

Someday; I am always learning.
On weekdays, I write from 9 to 5 at my desk in the office with a lovely view of the backyard.
For me, writing is the perfect occupation because it relies on my mind, not my unreliable body, and enables me to produce beautiful stories and poems.
I only take breaks for lunch and errands; some days there may be many, while on other days there is only lunch, but they are a welcome respite.
Venturing outside the house brings more than its fair share of careful considerations and social niceties.
My biggest problem is overcoming a deep-rooted focus on only my own concerns.
Opening up to other people has become easier, but I still sometimes have to work hard at it.
Besides, I am up to my ears in issues with depth perception, fine motor coordination, and basic problem-solving.
I do better some days than others depending on how I am handling my internal emotions.
I am always deeply affected by my emotional state, but I do not panic.

I work through it and move on.
The end of the day is my favorite part by far,
safe and sound at home, where I am in best
command of my every faculty.
I may still be a bit of a klutz, but at least I am
in an environment I can move about most
confidently.
My head hits the pillow and I eventually drift
off to sleep, relieved that the condition has
been managed for another day.
I look forward to what I can learn and
overcome tomorrow.

Escape to Imagination

The most frequent space I "inhabit" is inside my own mind.

This internal headspace has been my constant companion since I can remember.

It is with me wherever I go, filling up with daydreams at my writing desk, generating elaborate plots on grocery runs, even interrupting my sleep with the most compelling dreams.

No matter how hard I try, I can never turn it off; granted, I do not try to very often, but when I am sufficiently compelled to, I find it nearly impossible regardless.

I can become obsessed with the ideas I come up with, to the detriment of anything happening in reality.

I do like real life, but it can be seriously tedious at times.

My mind craves activity all day; I am trying to fill the void.

Even as I write this, I pause every few minutes because of yet another stray thought.

Like a cat pawing at string, I feel compelled to grasp at these dangling threads and follow

them to unknown wonders.
They are no substitute for good, long-lasting,
real world relationships, but, for me, they are
as welcome as old friends.

Finding My Way Through Emotions

It was almost impossible for me to navigate through my own emotions and process those of others when I was a child.
Emotional states did not register with me.
I felt broad sensations without clear origins.
Understanding happiness was never a problem, but seldom did I understand why people were so giddy.
Sadness, disappointment, anger; I knew the sensations, but not where they came from.
I believe the autism condition deadened the portion of my brain that registered facial expressions and associated emotions.
I could not figure out what other people were feeling and how to best respond to them.
Similarly, I had no words to express my own feelings.
I was frustrated often because my communication skills did not keep pace with my racing thoughts.
There was always more I wanted to say that I could not get out.

I always felt like I was going to explode if I was not understood soon.

With help from my patient parents and years of practice, I have gained a general understanding of emotions, I understand my own feelings more clearly and can express them, and I have learned how to recognize a wider range of emotions in others and respond appropriately.

I want to keep improving.

In Sickness

Recently, I was struck by illness.
It was a strain of a flu bug, which left me lying
low for weeks sapping my energy and
ambition, enough to confine me to my bed.
This was a reminder of the reckless approach I
sometimes take with my health.
I ignore what should be obvious signs there is
something wrong, push myself too hard
without slowing down or taking breaks,
wanting to fulfill all commitments.
I do not mention my anguish to my parents
until well after the initial symptoms first
appear.
These harmful habits contributed significantly
to my overall sorry state.
It is my own fault I end up in these
predicaments.
I am solely fixated on the task at hand and am
willing to let all other concerns fall to the
wayside.
I work from morning to late afternoon five
days a week, sometimes weekends as well
when necessary.
I do not like the feeling of wasted productivity,

which is, to me, the worst possible reality as a writer.

Every fiber of my being wanted to return to my normal habits of living.

I tried to keep working while sick, trying to compose a good paragraph, only to realize the most acceptable course was to let my body rest and heal, take care of itself simply and naturally.

I then concentrated on taking my medicine, drinking plenty of fluids, relaxing and not letting the misery of my situation fray my nerves too much.

The illness faded with time and my parents' tender care.

I soon returned to my life and writing as if no time had been lost.

Schooling at Home

Elementary school was not a perfect fit for me. The classroom environment was chaotic, and my physical, social, and emotional needs were not always satisfactorily met.

I liked going while I was able, I learned quite a bit about life and the world, and I made lots of great friends, but by the end of third grade, the wheels had come undone.

My parents decided to take me out, and from fourth grade until I turned 16, I took lessons at home, with my mom as my teacher.

She was demanding and honest, pushing me to bring out my best and show real aptitude within my schoolwork.

I was excited to learn all I could.

Nearly every day I learned something interesting and often invaluable to later endeavors.

The material was endlessly engaging; I sometimes stole another look at my textbooks to reexamine my favorite parts.

I still engaged in extracurricular activities: Physical and Occupational Therapies, Speech Therapy, dance class, Special Olympics, and other interests.

These were all holdovers from my elementary school days, crucial to my overall development and higher functioning.

The years flew by and I became more proficient at my studies.

Eventually my textbooks became less challenging, going over topics and problems I had already mastered.

The last year I was homeschooled proved especially disappointing, just one long review, nothing new.

It was satisfying to know that I was indeed familiar with all that my textbooks were reiterating, but also disappointing that they could not push me any further.

I moved on to studying for my GED.

This felt like a true challenge, the culmination of a lifetime of learning.

After nearly a year of intense studying, I took my GED test.

I was relieved when I passed with flying colors.

I moved on to college, but stayed at home for all of my online classes.

I had my reasons: traveling to the physical

campus would have proven difficult, and as I was already used to learning in the comfort of my own home, the option of online classes proved particularly enticing.

I was punctual, diligent, and to my mild surprise, given I was "attending" with virtual classrooms full of similar at-home students, quite social.

I greatly enjoyed my collegiate experience; my professors pushed me to expand my horizons, and I discovered many surprising things concerning the world and myself that I feel shaped my life's path in a positive direction.

I graduated with top marks, embarking on my writing career in short order.

I sometimes wonder if I could have handled traditional middle and high school life.

It likely would have been just as chaotic as third grade in elementary school, and who knows if I would have had the same opportunities, benefits, or experiences learning at home provided.

It is ultimately a moot point.

I feel my life has gone far better because of the path I have trod.

Finding My Voice

Because of my autism, I have been known to fixate on certain images, sounds, characters, and ideas for extraordinarily long periods of time, sometimes even years after I first encountered them.

They became part of my visual and verbal vocabulary and remain fixtures of how I think and express myself.

It started early: the engine noises of "Thomas & Friends," dead-on impressions of Cookie, Kermit, and Elmo, the deep thoughtful tones of Garfield the cat.

While finding my own voice, I "borrowed" those of others, shamelessly and with considerable glee.

They had ways of saying everything I felt with unerring clarity and signature personality.

I stuck to them far longer than I probably should have.

I grew more confident in my own powers of communication and was surprised that my voice could be just as strong as theirs, if not more so in crucial situations.

I sometimes feel a bit uncomfortable about it,

as it carries a lot of responsibility.
I have proven capable in a leadership position,
but I would rather take orders than give them.
Still, if I can make a positive difference, then I
will speak out for good causes every chance I
get, anywhere I can.

I can more than stand on my own.

What Am I Doing Here?

There are several possibilities, but I hesitate to
put all my eggs in one basket.
In one sense, I am just a person with autism
attempting to succeed in the best way I can.
In another, I am making a stand as a positive
example of a person living with this condition.
Furthermore, I am expressing hope
for millions of people who have been told
that their life choices are limited
for any number of reasons.
It could also be that I am simply trying
to make sense of my place in the world
and wanting to help others to find theirs.
I am in the thick of it all right now, and the
target keeps moving every day.
At any rate, I hope to live long enough to see
my work affect the world in a meaningful way.
There is more to be done, and many miles left
to log.

Fears

The dark of night is a prominent fear for me.
I feel better when I sleep with a night-light;
if I wake in the middle of the night, I like to
have a clear view of my surroundings.
I am no longer scared of "monsters" or outside
noises, but odd shadows and sudden
movements easily startle me.
I recently became somewhat of a world
traveler, a new reality with a growing list of
concerns.
I am afraid that if I go to another country, I
will not get back home.
I fear I would somehow be stuck in a legal
limbo, unable to provide adequate proof of my
identity or my reason for being there.
Strangely, I am fine with plane rides;
I know what I hear on the news, but all of my
flights have been successful.
I actually enjoy flying.
I feel the same about cars;
I enjoy riding.
I read, listen to the radio, and relax.
I have been in one car accident
which significantly impacted my life, but it

was a perfect storm of independent conditions
which led to that incident.

I have dealt with the flu, mosquitoes, and other
pests.

They have not killed me, but their drawbacks
are always on my mind, especially during the
seasons in which they are most prevalent and
widespread.

My greatest fear is that my life is changing too
fast.

I am not personally opposed to change
and I even enjoy new scenery or situations, but
I still have the lingering feeling that if I have
to adjust too quickly, I may be overwhelmed.

I have come close to breaking several times,
but I coped and everything worked out.

In the long run, I do not want to be defined by
my fears.

I want to manage them accordingly and live
life positively.

Did You Know You Were Autistic?

A question I have been asked several times.
At first, I was unaware.
In fact, I did not perceive much of anything, or
at least, I did not pay much attention to
anything in particular.
All I know for sure was that I lived in the
moment; every feeling and reaction was
immediate and intense.
My parents said the condition's name
countless times during discussions with
doctors, relatives, and friends, but they did not
directly discuss it with me.
I likely would not have understood what it
meant anyway.
Over the next few years, I noticed some things
that were unusual about my life compared to
other kids.
I learned, worked, and played with my
classmates, but I was often separated from
them to do tests on my own, go to therapy,
take speech classes, or do other activities.
I seldom took the bus for field trips and never

Feeling Frustration

When I was younger, almost everything felt
excessively hard for me to do.
I could not hold onto a pencil, walk a straight
line, speak my mind clearly and concisely.
I would lose my balance and fall a lot.
It was enough to make me feel like I wanted to
explode.
I went through the gamut of antisocial
behavior.
I bit, punched, kicked, pushed, pulled, and
shoved.
What I remember most, though, is the
screaming, my continuous shrieks for hours or
more, or simply groans, moans, and whines
until I was too exhausted to rebel anymore
or too hoarse from wearing out my throat.
It took me anywhere from a few moments to
calm down, to most of the day and sometimes
well beyond, during which time just the
feeling might be left and I had forgotten what I
was mad about in the first place.
My parents, teachers, and therapists gave me
many useful techniques for dealing with my
frustration.

I could count to ten, or one hundred for more trying times, slowly breathe in and out for a minute or two, and, once I had the capability to, talk through the cause of my rage with a trustworthy adult.

They worked wonderfully, curing me of my moping and returning me to a peaceful existence.

I have had many aggravating moments through the years, but I do not allow the feeling to linger.

I am aware of the negative effects of retaining anger, and I do not want to hurt more than I already have.

I know it is better to be calmer, and I can get more done with a clear mind.

I let the rage ebb away,   and get on with the rest of my day.

Playing the Game

I always liked playing board games.
Whenever life became too chaotic, when my
mood needed improving, gathering around the
table with family and friends to play a few
rounds of beloved games
or trying out new ones was a surefire cure-all
for me.
I spent many relaxing hours trying to get four
checkers in a row, pick small shapes out of
unusual body cavities with a pair of tweezers,
purchase properties and collect high rents,
solve a mysterious crime in a Victorian
mansion, and numerous other experiences.
I cherished my time with these games;
I loved recognizing regimented play patterns
with varying degrees of deviation, discovering
ways I could excel and maybe help other
players along.
They gave me the sense of structure,
organization, and equal rules I craved.
They helped me to realize the value of taking
turns, giving everyone a chance to make their
move.
Everyone had a fair chance to win, and even if

they did not, we all had good fun.

In a way, these games prepared me for life in the adult world.

I have had to come to grips with a complex set of rules, to understand a series of social interactions, and to be ready for unexpected events.

I still have a fondness for games.

My ever-growing "Monopoly" collection points to this passion.

"Clue" remains a big favorite, a test of logic and determination that I can never get enough of.

Games are a welcome diversion from a tough day, but also enriching experiences I can take with me through life.

Love in the Time of Autism

Love is a hard concept for me to describe,
much less understand.
It often does not register with me as strongly
or deeply as other sensations, except with my
parents or other loved ones.
I have genuine affection for my family and
certain others.
It is a warm, not quite fuzzy, but certainly a
comforting feeling, a mental hug upon first
contact with a familiar face.
I think this first developed in me as a form of
what some might call "loyalty."
I would rather chalk this feeling up to a kind
of metaphysical closeness, a spiritual bonding
beyond regular relationships.
I seldom use the word "intimate," but for such
an intense emotion, it would be appropriate
here.
It is all-encompassing, powerful, and personal.
Even then, sometimes I do not feel like I am
really there, in that moment, with these loved
ones.
It feels a little weird to me.
I am "right there" and "not there" all at once;

I am watching it happen to someone else, someone who looks like me, but is somehow not entirely me.

I am not certain why I feel this way.

It could be that I am just particular about how much of a sensation I want to feel, or I might have reservations concerning certain types of interaction I do not easily tolerate. Regardless, I do greatly appreciate genuine efforts of true affection and gravitate toward kindness and love as naturally as a plant toward light.

Love is an absolutely necessary function for my continued optimal health and happiness, a confirmation that all is going right and that tomorrow could and will, indeed, be brighter.

The Next Step

Figuring out where my life is going to go
has been a question I have worried about
ever since I began making efforts
to live more independently.
It has been an upward struggle
to even begin to maintain
a semblance of an everyday life.
I have achieved a degree of stability, but now
the problem becomes how to climb up to the
next strata.
I have identified a few goals which might
satisfactorily jumpstart my ascent, although
each comes with an asterisk.
One would be learning to operate a motor
vehicle.
This issue is a bit complex.
Many of my peers are able to drive, but I have
fears concerning my hand-eye coordination
and proper application of my motor skills.
Keeping my eyes on the road and both hands
on the wheel would be an incredibly
demanding prospect;
I could not guarantee full command of my
every motor faculty, and even a small-town

errand may demand much more than I could handle.

Another potential path to better living might be moving to a place of my own.

At some point, I may have to move away from my parents' orbit, live somewhere else where I can take care of my own needs.

This, of course, requires much more learning on my part.

I am still working on basic cooking skills; beyond making my own simplistic breakfast and lunch, I have yet to work on more elaborate meals, many recipes yet to learn.

I have worked with a stove and made breakfast on a waffle iron, but my repertoire is severely limited.

I do a decent job cleaning my parents' house; sweeping, vacuuming, and other odd chores come naturally to me now after years of practice.

The trick if I move to a new place will be to learn how to keep that locale spic and span as well, which I imagine should not be too taxing.

The supreme challenge, though, would be resisting the urge to just rely on my parents or another helper for the rest of my life.

I have always required assistance for seemingly every action at first, and even as I have gained more self-autonomy, some things are still beyond my present grasp.

I feel like I want to fly, but I know I still need training with my wings.

Focusing on my weaknesses while embracing my strengths;

I will keep fighting.

Go with the Flow

During my school days, I sometimes used a tool called a "mind map" which is supposed to help people organize their thoughts.
The version I used looked like a bubbly spider web, separate ideas contained in bubbles connected by thin lines representing relationships between two concepts.
I thought these looked remarkably similar to another planning tool somewhat amusingly titled a "flow chart."
More ideas associated by lines, but now illustrated along a clearly defined path, diverging only when an idea generated a tangential thought, which may itself start a new series of thoughts, continuously pouring outward like a river, but which, to me, seems built more like a brick wall.
It was a useful aid for its time and purpose, but I always seemed to be more preoccupied with following the paths each tangent traveled.
Tracking the progression of an idea from a tiny seed to a more comprehensive destination was more enjoyable to me than the task of actually making a flow chart.

Still, I learned how to do it and gained a better sense of how ideas can change, expand, and become more tangible.

This best explains how my brain processes information.

I tend to think of events as complex webs. Interconnected relationships, people, places, events, objects, and everything else, are mapped out in my mind in an ever-expanding matrix.

If I encounter anything in my internal database, a million related memories of other things spring up as well.

These associations strongly color my reactions to present stimuli, which can be a positive or negative response.

Sometimes they can take me out of the moment, make me concentrate on them rather than on my immediate situation.

I try to exercise some willpower and prevent this from happening, and for the most part I have been able to function just fine, but I can still be easily distracted.

Or should I say, "Caught in the web?"

I know I ought to not get bogged down with so much small stuff, to make the most of every moment and leave a positive impact on the here and now.

So new branches can be built.

Bubble

For most of my early childhood, I would
consider myself blissfully unaware
of the larger mechanics of my surrounding
world.
I concentrated on immediate concerns
such as learning in school, eating right,
playing with friends, taking care of my pet cat,
engaging in extracurricular activities, etc.
As I got older, I knew other things were going
on in the world, important, life-altering events
that likely affected my quality of life in ways I
was not aware of.
My parents purposely kept me isolated
because I might have gotten overwhelmed and
upset otherwise.
I did not start watching the evening news until
late in my middle school years, and even then,
only after I had sufficiently proven that I could
handle tragedies and solemn events with
appropriate responses.
Despite how grim the world might seem at
times, even if things look exceptionally bleak,
I maintain an optimistic view of life, serving
everyone with the best intent, putting my

greatest effort into everything I do, dedicating myself to getting the job done.

I now recognize the need to break out of the "bubble."

It is better for me to continue engaging with the world, to converse with and help all I can, to live life to the fullest and not forgetting to "pop the bubble."

Well-Read

One of the key moments of my development
was learning how to read on my own.
No one taught me; I just instinctively knew
how.
One of my earliest memories is reading "The
Cat in the Hat" to my grandma at bedtime.
Rather than the "normal" sight of the parent or
grandparent reading a story to lull the child to
sleep, I would read myself, and I always
wanted to read another.
Exciting stories filled my mind with wonder,
introducing me to people, places, and concepts
beyond what I could experience in my
hometown, sparking my imagination with
unexpected ingenuity, opening me up to new,
nearly limitless possibilities.
I soon became a voracious reader, carrying a
book everywhere I could.
In my early years, I could relate to books
better than I could with most people I knew.
I knew what book characters were thinking,
and I could safely assume what they might do
next.
Real-life people were much more complicated.

They were engaged in their own stories,
dealing with motivations and complications
which often escaped me.
Obviously, my story was intertwined with my
family's tale, but my parents had wider
perspectives than my much narrower reality,
and could see more elements that shaped my
story than I would have been able to
understand.
As time went on, I gained more "pages,"
a better understanding of how my story
was part of the story of the world at large.
I enjoyed being able to have a role in
something greater than my own sphere, to help
others achieve their hopes and dreams
and tell their own tales.
My love of stories even influenced my choice
of career.
I felt compelled to tell my own life story
in addition to others I had always wanted to
tell but never had the courage to try until I was
much older and more certain of my future
ambitions.
Putting words together to make vivid
tapestries of what had been formerly abstract
thought and highly personal experience

was oddly empowering and often enlightening for me.

I was able to make sense of a myriad of intense sensory experiences from across many years which I could seldom rationalize before. A whole world of communication and honesty was opened to me which I have embraced and pushed forward every day.

There are many stories I still wish to tell, and I hope in time you can hear them all.

Out of My Depth

Life with autism can sometimes lead to
moments of great trauma.
I vividly remember such a time from my
younger days.
I was part of a community swim program, an
effort to improve my muscle tone and physical
fitness as well as gain a useful life skill.
I actually enjoyed the class very much for
several reasons.
Some of my cousins and school friends were
classmates there.
My swim teacher was friendly and patient
and always encouraged me to do my best
at each swimming lesson.
The cool water of the pool felt relaxing to me,
and I enjoyed moving around in it.
However, there was one sticking point, one
action which gave me a great deal of anxiety.
It involved jumping into the shallow end of the
pool, a requirement as the swimming lessons
progressed.
I had always preferred to use the ladder
to lower myself into the pool
or slowly slide down from a sitting position

from the side.

I could control my descent and acclimate to the water on my own terms and in my own good time.

Jumping in, put briefly:

the exact opposite.

I stood on the edge of the pool's shallow end, looked straight down into the light blue abyss, and felt fear.

I stood stock still, staring endlessly at the pool's terrible expanse, unable to see the bottom, afraid to even dip a toe in lest I somehow trip and fall in.

My mother and my swim teacher tried to help me to overcome my irrational thinking, but my negative mindset felt more sensible than any case they could make.

Why was I so stubborn that day?

I imagined an image of a sheer cliff face, the kind Wile E. Coyote fell off and Simba's father was pushed into.

I also hated being completely submerged underwater.

I did not like my head or hair to get wet. Such a plunge as I was required to do at that moment would surely send me deep in an instant,completely covered in water, with no bottom to break my fall.

My poor mind could not handle this deadly combination of perceived threats.

Seeing my only option left was to completely shut down, I screamed loudly and repeatedly.

I refused to jump;

all attempts to break me out of my fearful state were to no avail.

The class ended, everyone else was leaving, but my mother and teacher insisted I complete the jump.

I came to the realization that I did not want to remain in this moment forever.

I took the plunge, hit the water, found the bottom, realized I could stand, knew I was safe.

I am much more comfortable in pools now.

That terrible fear can still come to mind, but I do not let it control me.

Delayed Reaction

When I was younger and the first symptoms of autism hit me, my parents observed I was noticeably slow to respond to them sometimes. They would talk to me or point to something they wanted me to look at, but I would either take some time to acknowledge them or simply ignore them altogether and concentrate on whatever I was doing.

This could be dangerous at times, such as when we crossed the road and I paid no attention to Mom's warnings that a car was coming.

For many years, she had to have a tight grip on me when out so I would not get hurt.

Trips to the grocery store were their own brand of chaos, where a thousand distractions could take a young boy away from his immediate surroundings, where this colorful magazine cover or that mascot-emblazoned food item was more important than staying at my parents' side or keeping an eye on the other shoppers so as to not accidentally bump into them.

My parents worked with me on improving my

reaction time, and Speech and Vision Therapy helped to correct many aspects of my inability to maintain overall awareness.

I am now able to focus my attention on what is around me, take better care of myself and others by watching where I am going, and make sense of everything I see.

The Writer's Petty Concerns

I write almost every day.
It is a therapeutic activity which helps me to work out worries and identify my hopes and dreams.
Whether forming a new poem, refining a speech, working on a blog post, creating my dream novel, or even writing a thank-you note, the very act of writing is, on the whole, deeply satisfying to me.
That being said, not every part of the writing process brings the same sense of accomplishment.
Sometimes, there is no getting around certain aspects of the job which can make my day harder.
When I am in the thick of work, I typically enter two states of mind.
Most of the time, I am on a roll, ideas flowing from my mind to my hands and onto the page without delay.
Then there are times I find myself in a creative slump, falling into a rut of indecisiveness.
I have written my characters into a corner without considering how they can escape, or I

have a nice series of actions or images laid out but no way to tie them all together.

When I am in such binds, my mind does not picture a blank so much as a block of black ink obscuring the next idea.

It is perfectly comfortable sitting there, waiting for me to catch up with it, while I fret about exactly what it is, how I can connect it with the others, and what are the best words to express it in a clear, understandable way.

Sometimes these come together quickly; when one detail makes sense, the rest are implied and fit perfectly.

Other concepts may be more abstract, harder to relate to real world experiences.

These problems have stymied me on countless occasions, but resolving them and making them work helps me to grow creatively and logistically.

Maintaining a high to perfect degree of accuracy is also a major concern for my writing.

My approach to writing is that of a nose-to-the-grindstone perfectionist.

It greatly irks me if a word is misspelled, a punctuation mark is out of place or missing, or if a sentence, paragraph, or even an entire page looks aesthetically just off somehow.

To me, it is like viewing a great painting only to notice an odd brushstroke, or a song with missing notes, or a city skyline absent an iconic landmark.

I would hardly call it a golden rule, but I desire to give my readers the confidence that what they are reading is professionally written, edited, and presented.

Anything less is unacceptable in my eyes.

I want to always put my best foot forward.

Staying motivated during a writing project is also a concern.

Sitting in front of a computer screen for an extended time, focused on a singular writing endeavor, is a significant commitment.

With some projects, this time can be a joyful, highly productive stretch in which I am fully invested in the work and at the peak of my creative ability, as excited to complete the work as I want my readers to be when they have it in their hands.

Nothing could keep me away from my writing desk.

Other days are a bit more of a slog.

I remain dedicated to diligently plugging away at my various projects.

Of course, my professional obligations outweigh any personal criticisms or protestations I may have.

I am obligated to render the best service I am able.

If I can satisfy the needs of my audience, then my efforts have been worthwhile.

Any annoyances I experience are temporary, and, I refuse to let them affect the quality of my work, or my life.

An Acquired Taste

My autism and my senses are closely linked.
My direct perception of everything in the
world is filtered through selective lenses
which I fight to control.
I have made adjustments to my life and have
had many therapies to compensate for what
my brain misses, but some areas are still
difficult to negotiate, which can greatly upset
me.
One difficult sensory component in my life
is dealing with different food textures.
This has dogged me almost from birth.
The lingering effects of a difficult texture and
a bad taste in my mouth is one sensation I can
readily recall.
My mother has told me that when I was a
baby, I ate baby food without complaint.
The problems started when she tried to switch
me to regular table food.
Suddenly, the way certain foods felt in my
mouth became overwhelming.
Peas were bumpy orbs that never sat perfectly;
I was never quite sure how to best approach
them.

Cooked, sliced carrots were a favorite, but in raw, uncut form, they were too big and hard.

Mashed potatoes went down fine, but spaghetti was too messy.

My usual reaction to a challenging texture would be to gag and vomit.

My mother continued to introduce new foods as I grew.

It was an ongoing effort to expand my diet, and my diet did expand.

I acquired a tolerance for different textures, sometimes quickly, other times taking years of repeated exposure.

I enjoy a number of different foods and textures now.

I still remain sensitive to how certain foods feel which can trigger negative reactions, but I experience them far less often.

I have developed a more sophisticated palate and plan on expanding my food horizons further.

Imagination and Compromise

My mind has always been unbelievably active.
Rarely is it quiet or not brimming with ideas.
I am grateful for this trait as a constant engine
of inspiration for my writing and my life in
general.
However, there have been times when I let my
imagination run away from me, fly a bit too
freely, and it has disrupted other activities or
taken me away from more pressing concerns.
When I was younger and less inclined to
consider forces beyond what lay in front of
me, my inner mindscape was filled to the brim
with an odd mixture of real-life memories
and characters from television, films, and
books.
My already-tenuous connection to reality was
further muddled by an inability to separate
media from message.
As far as I was concerned, on-screen
happenings were more vibrant, engaging, and
frankly, important.
I paid attention to what characters were saying
and doing more than what was going on
around me.

This became a problem in school and other social settings as I spent more time maintaining imaginary adventures and making sure they were consistent in my mind from day to day when I should have been concentrating on homework, chores, conversations, or other concerns.

The worlds and scenarios I created were empowering and intoxicating to me in ways that the real world could not readily supply. My parents never allowed me to entertain such notions for very long, always bringing me back to the present moment before I was completely lost to the illusions.

They helped me to structure my day so that my time was mainly occupied with creative pursuits, extracurricular activities, and other things which would displace obsessive media from my mind.

I still like movies, television, and video games, and I have always been a voracious reader. Through reading, I gained an appreciation for history and geography in general, and language arts and writing in particular. These helped me make exciting discoveries about my world and myself, and gave me inspiration to open myself up more to the world.

I still think about what I watch sometimes, but I am more preoccupied with sharing my experiences and telling compelling stories based on people, places, and things I love. Every day I work on these is a new day of self-discovery, a chance for me to add to the collection of wonderful stories I and others continue to enjoy and hopefully benefit from well into the future.

Relapse

There are times when I struggle with certain behavioral tics or, as some would say, stims. I am not intentionally trying to do such things, but I tend to carry them out reflexively, with hardly any thought put behind them.
They are mostly comprised of habits I keep thinking I can control.
Sometimes I have done so for years, but, to my surprise and consternation, they can recur at inopportune moments.
For instance, during times of frustration, I resist the urge to bite my hand, a self-harming habit my parents worked hard to stop me from repeating.
I know it causes me physical pain, leaves embarrassing teeth marks on my skin, and is far too childish for someone my age to exhibit.
Still, I have moments of weakness when I forget all of that, give in to the emotion and bite, giving me the most immediate relief I can think of.
All my tensions are concentrated and simultaneously relieved in that one moment as I bite down.

More often I can just think through my frustration, identify the source of my agony, and deal with it accordingly.

After all, I cannot allow my feelings regarding every obstacle I hit to affect everything I do and prevent anything meaningful from getting done.

I also do not want to hurt myself.

I likewise have a tendency to talk to myself.

I have often imitated the voices of my favorite characters from television and films.

I have a good ear for picking up on the unique inflections and tones certain voices possess, and can effectively mimic them with a fair degree of accuracy.

This was my favorite pastime, an evergreen entertainment source, powered by my own imagination.

Of course, it was also one which distracted and took my mind away from what needed to be done, a flaw in logical thinking and what proved to be a serious detriment as the circumstances of my life and my responsibilities that came with them grew.

It took a long time for me to break this habit, or at least to reduce it to a less frequent

occurrence where it would not disrupt my
daily activity.

I still impersonate from time to time, but never
to the point of nuisance.

I like being in control and do not want to get
pulled away and lost in my own addictive
stimuli.

Dedication and Perseverance

My personal motto is "Never give up."
It permeates every corner of my life.
There have been times when it seemed, to my
limited view at least, that the goal appeared
too far off, my current circumstances too
binding.
During these periods, it became crucial that I
keep my temper, stay the course, find resolve,
keep my gaze on my goal until I either
achieved it or found a more worthwhile
pursuit.
Often, I find that the experience of facing the
problem head-on and learning from it is just as
rewarding as the destination itself.
As I have gotten older, I have found myself
accepting more risk and taking on greater
challenges, but not experiencing as much
stress as I did in the past.
When I was far younger, I experienced a great
deal of anxiety any time I stepped outside my
comfort zone, usually accompanied by a
queasiness which I could barely contain.
The very thought of trying something new was
often enough for my body to instantly revolt.

It took some serious convincing by my parents for me to realize and firmly believe that my wild rationalizations had no basis in reality. Once I moved past my own reservations, I found these new experiences to be fun, engaging, and well worth my participation. Now, I do register a bit of nervousness at the start of major new ventures, but not to the extent that the feeling debilitates me.

In a sense, the most powerful force in my day-to-day existence is the desire to finish what I set out to do, or at least make it closer to the conclusion.

This usually means chipping away at whatever task I engage in.

I am in far better control of my faculties, more mentally hardy and committed to fulfilling my obligations each day.

Such a reality is welcome and worked for, one I can live up to every time.

Feet Defeat

Where lies my breaking point?
What has given me more grief and aggravation
compared to any other sensory irritant?
It has haunted me always.
I am terribly sensitive about anyone touching
my feet, especially around my toes.
Even wearing my sneakers, or looking down
at my toes in my sneakers can trigger this
irritant; all this discomfort can be exacerbated
by people touching my toes, or about to touch
them.
There is one somewhat psychological reason
that may explain why I feel this way.
When I was a little boy, I looked almost
exclusively down at my feet all the time as I
walked.
I seldom looked ahead, obsessed with the very
act of taking forward steps and seeing how my
feet coped with different surfaces, hills, dips,
and obstructions in my path, always staring at
my feet and the ground ahead, trying not to
trip and fall.
My gross motor issues made every step an
uncertainty.

Every time I walked, I would shakily transport myself and often required help from my parents or someone I trusted.
Because of my problems walking and keeping my balance, I was afraid that someone would hurt my feet and I would never walk again.

Whenever my feet were approached by human hands, this feeling was most prominent in my mind.
When my parents and I shopped for my new sneakers and the store employee wanted to see if they fit snugly all the way to the toe, I could see the hand coming from miles away.
And every time, I instinctively flinched.
Squeezing my toes into a tight space was more than enough to upset me and make me cry uncontrollably.
In an attempt to ease my distress, my parents insisted on helping me at the shoe store themselves.
This had decidedly mixed results; I did not complain nearly as much, but I was still unusually sensitive about my toes being touched and would curl them inward and turn my foot away.

Even just thinking about it as I write this creates discomfort and causes me to cringe, as automatic a reflex as I have ever had.

It strikes me that I may also be experiencing an extreme sensory reaction regarding touch on my feet and toes.

The powerful combo of fear and sensitivity can be overwhelming.

It is as if the sensation of discomfort is hard-wired into the nerves of my feet.

I wish I could better control my foot-related anguish, channel more willpower into ignoring this baser instinct.

After all, in my everyday experience, getting used to footwear, having it fit well, and leaving for daily engagements in a timely manner, is a practical necessity.

I suppose I do not find my momentary discomfort too debilitating, but I would be interested in seeing if I can somehow overcome or curtail it.

My feet certainly would not complain.

For Every Street I Cross

For every street I crossed without looking both
ways before I could do it safely.
For every time I overcompensated for what I
thought were difficult tasks until I learned
ways to accomplish them.
For all the times I was reminded to make good
eye contact and listen carefully and all the
wonderful things I discovered when I did so.
For the countless hours in therapy and speech
without which I might have never been able to
completely function.
For all the great friends I made in school and
in life and for those who taught me how to
make friends and keep them for life.
For every time I have been told, "Let's try
again," and, "Don't give up. You can do it."
For all the credit I have to give to the support
team of my parents, teachers, family and
friends who have believed in me and helped
me to take my own first steps into the world.
My love, appreciation, and respect for you all
knows no bounds.
For every street I cross, because you show me
the way.

A Conversation

When I am speaking with you, my mind is
processing many things.
I am trying to maintain eye contact.
I am concentrating on what you are saying.
I try to come up with an appropriate response.
Sometimes you go too fast, or I am distracted
by another thought, or our discussion takes an
odd turn, leaving me at a loss for words, but
only for a moment or two.
I do enjoy repartee, but for me, it does not
come easily.
Sometimes when we converse, I say things I
later regret.
At the time, I thought they were suitable, but
only after we are through do I realize the way I
worded it was not what I intended or that you
might have been offended.
By this time, when it is too late, we have
moved on to other things, and I am too
embarrassed or caught up in my own thoughts
to track you down again and clarify or
apologize, it hurts me inside, more than it
probably should, because in my mind, I tend to
turn molehills into mountains.

Puzzle

I like the thought of one of autism's symbols
being a puzzle piece.
My life sometimes feels like a series of
puzzles, or maybe a large one with many parts.
Either way, trying to put my life in order, and
keeping it together, is a full-time job.
A pile of pieces can make me excited, but also
a bit anxious.
So many pieces, too many similar shades of
color.
"Where do they all go?" I think.
Putting the "frame" together first is the most
important part for me; without the corner and
border pieces in place, I feel lost.
Similarly, my life is "framed" by my family,
my home, and the values I cherish.
Placing all the difficult pieces of my life
within this "frame" helps me to maintain a
sense of normalcy.
Physical issues, from movement to vision and
more, affect me on a daily basis.
I find it hard to put names to faces at times,
even with people I know well.
Some everyday activities are difficult because

I forget some steps.

Sometimes I just completely "zone out," for reasons I cannot always explain.

Every day it seems I have at least one moment like this.

Life does not always make sense to me, but I do my best to get along with everyone and accomplish what needs doing.

Making sense of chaos and restoring order, putting the world back together as it should be, makes me feel better, especially once I have gotten all the pieces in place.

My life is full of endless puzzles, mysteries, and riddles.

I can solve some on my own, but I need help with others.

Once I figure them out, though, my anxiety disappears.

I welcome each one as it comes, as I come closer to completing my life's puzzle.

Autism

Awakening to this reality was scary at first,
not so much now

Understanding the effects of this condition is
an ongoing process

Timid nature from the start, but confidence
came as barriers fell away

Intelligence helps immensely; now if only I
wasn't so weak physically

Senses are hyperactive, generally functional,
slightly unfocused

My outlook remains sunny; I work to clear
the clouds

Awareness

Acknowledgement of my limits and
overcoming them continues

Working toward acceptance in the wider
world is rewarding, too

Actions in positive directions remove the
negative stigma one piece at a time

Repeating mistakes is common in my life;
I'd like to stop them

Education continues on life skills and new
ways to live with the condition

Never thought I would survive this long, I
think to myself at the start of some days

Extreme emotional reactions used to be
frequent, still happen sometimes

Slowing down and taking in all details has
greatly helped

Stopped to see how far I have to go; I like
my chances, I keep walking on

And Now

The author, Benjamin Kellogg, hopes that you have enjoyed reading his poems.

Please tell people about this eBook, or write a review on your favorite social networking site.

You may also be interested in Benjamin's "Noah and Logan Children's Book Series". Illustrated Children's stories focusing on the social skills that he struggled with as a child, available from Amazon.

CPSIA information can be obtained
at www.ICGtesting.com
Printed in the USA
LVHW020236061120
670809LV00007B/1000

9 781916 494442